Relations

A. K. RAMANUJAN

Relations

POEMS

LONDON
OXFORD UNIVERSITY PRESS
NEW YORK   BOMBAY
1971

Oxford University Press, Ely House, London W.1
GLASGOW NEW YORK TORONTO MELBOURNE WELLINGTON
CAPE TOWN DELHI IBADAN NAIROBI DAR ES SALAAM LUSAKA ADDIS ABABA
BOMBAY CALCUTTA MADRAS KARACHI LAHORE DACCA
KUALA LUMPUR SINGAPORE HONG KONG TOKYO

ISBN 0 19 211810 2

© Oxford University Press 1971

*Printed in Great Britain by
The Bowering Press Plymouth*

for

MOLLY
KRITTIKA
KRISHNA

*Like a hunted deer
on the wide white
salt land,*

    *a flayed hide
    turned inside out,*

*one may run,
escape.*

    *But living
among relations
binds the feet.*

        From a Classical Tamil Anthology
        (1st–3rd century A.D.)

ACKNOWLEDGEMENTS

Acknowledgements are due to the editors of the following anthologies and periodicals in which some of these poems first appeared: *The Chicago Review, The Illustrated Weekly of India, Indian Writing Today, New York Times, Pergamon Poets, Quest*; also to the following radio and TV stations: WFMT (Chicago), WKPK (Chicago), All India Radio (Delhi, Bangalore), and New Delhi TV.

Among my conscious debts are a phrase from Vinda Karandikar (page 22), one from Pablo Neruda's prose (page 20), and an incident from a Kannada magazine story (page 51).

CONTENTS

It does not Follow, but when in the Street	1
Man and Woman in Camera and Out	2
A Wobbly Top	4
Of Mothers, among other things	5
The Hindoo: he doesn't Hurt a Fly, or a Spider either	6
Time and Time Again	8
Love Poem for a Wife. 1	9
Routine Day Sonnet	12
Army Ants	13
One, Two, maybe Three, Arguments against Suicide	15
One more after reading Homer	17
Some Indian Uses of History on a Rainy Day	18
A Lapse of Memory	20
Eyes, Ears, Noses, and a Thing about Touch	21
The Hindoo: he reads his Gita and is calm at all events	23
Poona Train Window	24
Time to Stop	26
Love Poem for a Wife. 2	27
Entries for a Catalogue of Fears	30
The Hindoo: the Only Risk	34
Real Estate	35
Any Cow's Horn can do it	37
When it Happens	39
Small-scale Reflections on a Great House	40

Smalltown, South India	44
Some Relations	45
Take Care	47
The Last of the Princes	49
Old Indian Belief	50
History	51
Compensations	53
Obituary	55
Prayers to Lord Murugan	57

IT DOES NOT FOLLOW, BUT WHEN IN THE STREET

yellow trees bend over broken glass
and the walls of Central Jail
drip with spring's laburnum
yellows, yellow on yellow,

I forget the eczema on my feet,
the two holes in my shoe: at once I know
I'll have a sharp and gentle daughter,
an old age somewhere; I walk on air,

I walk on water, can even bear
to walk on earth for my wife
and I will someday somehow share

a language, a fire, a clean first floor
with a hill in the window; and eat
on an ancient sandalwood door.

MAN AND WOMAN IN CAMERA AND OUT

In the small bright square
of the viewfinder
one image slurs another.

I try to match the circle
with the square, play
at the hocuspocus

of man, tree, and door,
peeking in and out
of the black box

with left eye and right
eye and the eye in between,
screwing them high and low,

fingering the focus,
reading the obvious light
by digits, the blind

feeling the blind,
knowing light by heat
and a wall by the wind,

till by a tiny act
of grace multiples
jell to a duplicate,

half man, half tree,
the left above the right,
they slide to meet

in a symmetry
of two eyes in a face,
the circle in the square

no enlargement of nose
or liver, but lifesize, exact,
small as the rest of him,

brown man in dotted tie
and five o'clock shadow,
the cherry tree behind

in bloom, not loosened yet
as it would be tomorrow.
With a click of luck

I married him then,
married a focus, now
a photograph in a frame

on the table in my living room,
while he himself goes
in and out of sight,

smooth by morning,
hairy by night,
growing from blur

to focus and back.

A WOBBLY TOP

At times, the wobbly top father gave me
quietly, after we both had a tantrum,

suddenly begins to spin so fast it's still:
every scar on its body now describes

a perfect circle within other scars'
perfect concentric circles, as in

a time-exposure of the sky.

OF MOTHERS, among other things

I smell upon this twisted
blackbone tree the silk and white
petal of my mother's youth.
From her ear-rings three diamonds

splash a handful of needles,
and I see my mother run back
from rain to the crying cradles.
The rains tack and sew

with broken thread the rags
of the tree-tasselled light.
But her hands are a wet eagle's
two black pink-crinkled feet,

one talon crippled in a garden-
trap set for a mouse. Her sarees
do not cling: they hang, loose
feather of a onetime wing.

My cold parchment tongue licks bark
in the mouth when I see her four
still sensible fingers slowly flex
to pick a grain of rice from the kitchen floor.

THE HINDOO: he doesn't Hurt a Fly or a Spider either

It's time I told you why
I'm so gentle, do not hurt a fly.

Why, I cannot hurt a spider
either, not even a black widow,

for who can tell Who's Who?
Can you? Maybe it's once again my

great swinging grandmother,
and that other (playing at

patience centered in his web)
my one true ancestor,

the fisherman lover who waylaid her
on the ropes in the Madras harbour,

took her often from behind
imprinting on her face and body

(not to speak of family tree
or gossip column)

lasting impressions of his net:
till, one day, spider-

fashion, she clamped down and bit
him while still inside her,

as if she'd teeth down there—
they'd a Latin name for it,

which didn't help the poor man one bit.

And who can say I do not bear,
as I do his name, the spirit

of Great Grandfather, that still man,
untimely witness, timeless eye,

perpetual outsider,
watching as only husbands will

a suspense of nets vibrate
under wife and enemy

with every move of hand or thigh:
watching, watching, like some

spider-lover a pair
of his Borneo specimens mate

in murder, make love with hate,
or simply stalk a local fly.

TIME AND TIME AGAIN

Or listen to the clocktowers
of any old well-managed city

beating their gongs round the clock, each slightly
off the others' time, deeper or lighter

in its bronze, beating out a different
sequence each half-hour, out of the accidents

of alloy, a maker's shaking hand
in Switzerland, or the mutual distances

commemorating a donor's whim,
the perennial feuds and seasonal alliance

of Hindu, Christian, and Muslim—
cut off sometimes by a change of wind,

a change of mind, or a siren
between the pieces of a backstreet quarrel.

One day you look up and see one of them
eyeless, silent, a zigzag sky showing

through the knocked-out clockwork, after a riot,
a peace-march time bomb, or a precise act

of nature in a night of lightnings.

LOVE POEM FOR A WIFE. 1

Really what keeps us apart
at the end of years is unshared
childhood. You cannot, for instance,
meet my father. He is some years
dead. Neither can I meet yours:
he has lately lost his temper
and mellowed.

In the transverse midnight gossip
of cousins' reunions among
brandy fumes, cashews and the Absences
of grandparents, you suddenly grow
nostalgic for my past and I
envy you your village dog-ride
and the mythology

of the seven crazy aunts.
You begin to recognize me
as I pass from ghost to real
and back again in the albums
of family rumours, in brothers'
anecdotes of how noisily
father bathed,

slapping soap on his back;
find sources for a familiar
sheep-mouth look in a sepia wedding
picture of father in a turban,
mother standing on her bare
splayed feet, silver rings
on her second toes;

and reduce the entire career
of my recent unique self
to the compulsion of some high
sentence in His Smilesian diary.
And your father, gone irrevocable
in age, after changing everyday
your youth's evenings,

he will acknowledge the wickedness
of no reminiscence: no, not
the burning end of the cigarette
in the balcony, pacing
to and fro as you came to the gate,
late, after what you thought
was an innocent

date with a nice Muslim friend
who only hinted at touches.
Only two weeks ago, in Chicago,
you and brother James started
one of your old drag-out fights
about where the bathroom was
in the backyard,

north or south of the well
next to the jackfruit tree
in your father's father's house
in Aleppiy. Sister-in-law
and I were blank cut-outs
fitted to our respective
slots in a room

really nowhere as the two of you
got down to the floor to draw
blueprints of a house from memory
on everything, from newspapers
to the backs of envelopes
and road-maps of the United States
that happened

to flap in the other room
in a midnight wind: you wagered heirlooms
and husband's earnings on what
the Uncle in Kuwait
would say about the Bathroom
and the Well, and the dying,
by now dead,

tree next to it. Probably
only the Egyptians had it right:
their kings had sisters for queens
to continue the incests
of childhood into marriage.
Or we should do as well-meaning
hindus did,

betroth us before birth,
forestalling separate horoscopes
and mothers' first periods,
and wed us in the oral cradle
and carry marriage back into
the namelessness of childhoods.

ROUTINE DAY SONNET

For me a perfectly ordinary
day at the office, only a red lorry
past the window at two;
a sailor with a chest tattoo.

A walk before dark
with my daughter to mark
another cross on the papaya tree;
dinner, coffee, bedtime story

of dog, bone and shadow. A bullock cart
in an Eskimo dream. But I wake with a start
to hear my wife cry her heart

out as if from a crater
in hell: she hates me, I hate her,
I'm a filthy rat and a satyr.

ARMY ANTS

The army ants not only make their houses but they are their house, for of their own living bodies they form the whole complicated dwelling.
C. Judson Herrick, *The Thinking Machine*

    Ancestors give them aristocratic tastes:
        separate apartments
        for the queen,
        colonies

        for the various castes,
        several nurseries
        for the abstract

        and the bean-eyed young,
        hung perhaps with tigerheads
        of red wild ants

for trophies, or for vitamins.

        Army ants build each builder
        for a brick, altar
        and martyr in one,

        or a tile on the floor,
        part of the prize decor
        for the bedroom

        of their most illustrious queen
        where slow males
        die young

or live older than death in nurseries of eggs.

>   Extremists, true makers
>   of made things, they have
>   only themselves
>
>   for bricks; knees for hinges; heads
>   for the plinths of their rain-
>   soaked Corinths;
>
>   the rafter a chainmail of stares
>   and the running
>   runway

a crazy pavement of hands and feet.

>   Not like the Great Wall of China
>   cemented with slave
>   and enemy
>
>   and the favourite almost dead;
>   the living, the young,
>   are the brick
>
>   and the mortar of this house
>   without legend.
>   And the work,

as they say, is the workman at last.

ONE, TWO, MAYBE THREE, ARGUMENTS AGAINST SUICIDE

1

Don't forget, dear departing saint:
you see red, you faint, at the sight
of blood. And there's always the danger
you may be understood, as never
     before, misconstrued by some
     casual stranger. Your bluebeard
     motives all over the toilet floor,
     only your lifelong good name will go
to hell: the rest of you, wrapped
in kitchen-cloth bandages, waits
in line, in a one-bulb lawcourt
with in-laws for lawyers; your poor heart
     pounds on hospital images,
     tetanus, the bluntness of knives,
     the corpse's nose-hair, and how awful
     if found dead in such yellowed underwear.

2

Better not attempt that suicide,
for you may find you've already died

and there's nothing left to kill.
Worse still, you may die formally

now, yet live on forever in spite
of what those doctors certify:

your self now a mere odourless soul,
a see-through man-shaped hole

in the air, a late lamenting ghost
looking in vain for an empty seat

at the full house of your posthumous
fame where you can see but not hear

the rain of applause, the jangle
of medals on the breast of your happy

unhappy widow. Though you're there
you wish you really were, wish the rain

or a touch of that intangible breast,
even that garden hose full blast

on the rosebush would quench the icy fire,
the love you hate, that burns, consumes, yet leaves

you whole.

3

Desire, bodiless, is endless.
Remember what the wise callous hindus

said when the love-god burned: keep your cool,
make for love's sake no noble gesture.

All symbol, no limbs, a nobody all soul,
O Kama, only you can have no use

for the *Kamasutra*.
                    Ashes have no posture.

ONE MORE AFTER READING HOMER

any cassandra with some e s p
can see the smoke grow thick
between her and the city faces
but she cannot show the sceptic

the brands in the marketplace.
cats in the alley may watch
the Stranger and walk close
to his knee to arch the fur

on their backs and mimic
the strut of later centurions.
cats being cats will purr
at all sorts of occult things

including a faint tattoo
on a great big wooden horse
getting wet in the rain.
neither paris nor cassandra

but only incurious cat   I come
upon a half-burned shoulderblade
greening in a lake of dead alewives
among leftovers papercups and condoms.

I wonder if in chicago too
love indifference and hate
in some devious way relate
at all to deaths by fire.

SOME INDIAN USES OF HISTORY ON A RAINY DAY

1

Madras,
        1965, and rain.
Head clerks from city banks
curse, batter, elbow
in vain the patchwork gangs
of coolies in their scramble
for the single seat
in the seventh bus:

they tell each other how
Old King Harsha's men
beat soft gongs
to stand a crowd of ten
thousand monks
in a queue, to give them
and the single visiting Chinaman
a hundred pieces of gold,
a pearl, and a length of cloth;

so, miss another bus, the eighth,
and begin to walk, for King Harsha's
monks had nothing but their own two feet.

2

Fulbright Indians, tiepins of ivory,
colour cameras for eyes, stand every July
in Egypt among camels,

faces pressed against the past
as against museum glass,
tongue tasting dust,

amazed at pyramidfuls
of mummies swathed in millennia
of Calicut muslin.

3

1935. Professor of Sanskrit
on cultural exchange;
                    passing through; lost
in Berlin rain; reduced
to a literal, turbanned child,
spelling German signs on door, bus, and shop,
trying to guess *go* from *stop*;
                    desperate
for a way of telling apart
a familiar street from a strange,
or east
from west at night,
the brown dog that barks
from the brown dog that doesn't,

memorizing a foreign paradigm
of lanterns, landmarks,
a gothic lotus on the iron gate;

suddenly comes home
in English, gesture, and Sanskrit,
assimilating
            the swastika
on the neighbour's arm
in that roaring bus from a grey
nowhere to a green.

A LAPSE OF MEMORY

As there are such things as the liar's
use of truth, and the well man's use
of illness, there must be an amnesiac

use of memory.
                After the lightning
strikes the tree and takes all the leaves,
an amnesiac may break into hives

but recognize nothing present
to his concave eye groping only
for mother and absences. Nothing

at all is family now to that estrangement:
neither the squares of office, nor round wife,
nor oblong home address with two

initials and a lifelong name. Friends
and family doctors hope he'll recover
all pasts and circulation of sap

back into fingertips through one crack
or lapse of memory somewhere in the inverse
branching under the earth. Maybe all it takes

is the smell of a woman's perfume
in a childhood latrine, a peanut seller's
raucous cry, or three obscene lines

mating white and black lizards
in schoolbook Sanskrit. Or a slant
of rain on the sunshine and the papaya tree.

EYES, EARS, NOSES, AND A THING ABOUT TOUCH

Eyes are fog,
are trees green or on fire,
a man's face quartered by the cross-
hairs of a gunsight. Crows, scarecrows,
eyes in others' eyes. A brown dog
dipped and gilded in the sunshine,
or blurred through someone else's glasses.

When lucky
it dawns birdcries,
the ear has children with bells;
the fall, delay, and fall
of a wooden doll on the wooden
stairs, what mother says
to cook and early beggar.

Urine on lily,
women's odours
in the theatre, a musk cat's
erection in the centre of a zoo,
the day's bought flowers
crushed into a wife's night
of grouses: the sudden happiness

of finding
where noses can go.
Touch alone has untouchables,
lives continent in its skin, so
segregating the body
even near is too far.
Through all things that press,

claw, draw blood,
yet do not touch,
it remembers a wet mouth
on a dry; clammy hands and tactless
manoeuvres on the ironwork
with the dew on the iron
in the two o'clock woods;

the burr I plucked
from your back's hollow,
the six, or eight, light
hairy legs of the tree spider
that walked the small of my back
and gave me a rash
for seven whole days.

THE HINDOO: he reads his GITA and is calm at all events

At this party heads have no noses, teeth close
upon my heart: yet I come unstuck
and stand apart. I do not marvel
when I see good and evil: I just walk

over the iridescence
of horsepiss after rain. Knives, bombs, scandal,
and cowdung fall on women in wedding lace:
I say nothing, I take care not to gloat.

I've learned to watch lovers without envy
as I'd watch in a bazaar lens
houseflies rub legs or kiss. I look at wounds calmly.

Yet when I meet on a little boy's face
the prehistoric yellow eyes of a goat
I choke, for ancient hands are at my throat.

POONA TRAIN WINDOW

I look out the window.

See a man defecating
between two rocks, and a crow.

Drink my railway tea.
A milestone newly
painted orange, black

numbers on its sides.
The blinding noise
and the afterhush
of one train passing

another, rise and fall
of hills in two sets
of windows, faces, a rush
of whole children, white
hair in a red turban.

I drink my railway tea.
Three women with baskets
on their heads, climbing
slowly against the slope
of a hill, one of them
lop-sided, balancing

between the slope and
the basket on the head
a late pregnancy.
Buffaloes swatting flies
with their tails.

Six gulls. The tea
darkens like a sick
traveller's urine.
Six gulls sitting still,

six eggs laid new
on grass, in, on, near,
water. I see a man

between two rocks.
I think of the symmetry

of human buttocks.

TIME TO STOP

There are times
           when
going to museums
makes you see

pointilliste anthills,

Picasso faces on milkmen
framed in the living room
window,

        a violet shadow
all around a dead
or dying cow
           and you come
back at night to see
how it looks
under the gaslight,

and after an accident,
              blood
looks remarkably
like fresh paint.

          Then
it's time to stop
going to museums.

LOVE POEM FOR A WIFE. 2

After a night of rage
that lasted days,
quarrels in a forest,
waterfalls, exchanges, marriage,
exploration of bays
and places
we had never known
we would ever know,

my wife's always
changing syriac face,
chosen of all faces,
a pouting difficult child's
changing in the chameleon
emerald
wilderness of Kerala,
small cousin to tall

mythic men, rubberplant
and peppervine,
frocks with print patterns
copied locally
from the dotted
butterfly,
grandmother wearing white
day and night in a village

full of the colour schemes
of kraits and gartersnakes;
adolescent in Aden among stabbing
Arabs, betrayed and whipped
yet happy among ships
in harbour,

and the evacuees,
the borrowed earth

under the borrowed trees;
taught dry and wet,
hot and cold
by the monsoons then,
by the siroccos now
on copper
dustcones, the crater
townships in the volcanoes

of Aden:
        I dreamed one day
that face my own yet hers,
with my own nowhere
to be found;   lost;   cut
loose like my dragnet
past.
I woke up and groped,
turned on the realism

of the ceiling light,
found half a mirror
in the mountain cabin
fallen behind the dresser
to look at my face now
and the face
of her sleep, still asleep
and very syriac on the bed

behind: happy for once
at such loss of face,
whole in the ambivalence

of being halfwoman half-
man contained in a common
body,
androgynous as a god
balancing stillness in the middle

of a duel to make it dance:
soon to be myself, a man
unhappy in the morning
to be himself again,
the past still there,
a drying
net on the mountain,

in the morning, in the waking
my wife's face still fast
asleep, blessed as by
butterfly, snake, shiprope,
and grandmother's other
children,
by my only love's only
insatiable envy.

ENTRIES FOR A CATALOGUE OF FEARS

1

Though I cannot always tell a fear
from a hope or a hope from a face
in the window
of a house on fire,
I know
fears far more precise
than any hope.
Born blind, a whole skin listening
and a seeing ear,
they do not have to grope.

2

Add now, at thirty-nine, to the old old fear
of depths and heights,
of father in the bedroom,
insects, iodine
in the eye,
sudden knives and urchin laughter
in the redlight alley,
add now
the men in line
behind my daughter.

3

My delicate
nails grow long
during a public lecture
and no one will hear me for
the noise of rustling nails nor
see my face

for the rivalry of their silicate
tangle.

4

I'll grow
charitable one day,
begin to classify
at dawn the week's breadcrumbs
in a plastic bag for the red and black
street ant,
the beggardoves in the park:
the free sapphire bluejay
in the tree
will make a habit
of the shelled peanut
in my hand.

5

Sixty, and one glass eye,
even I talk now and then of God,
find reasons to be fair
everywhere
to the even and to the odd,
see karma
in the fall of a tubercular sparrow,
in the newspaper deaths in Burma
of seventy-one men, women and children;
actually see the One in the Many,
losing a lifetime of double vision
with one small adjustment
of glasses.

6

Like any honest
man, unnerved by the slightest
inquiry into his flawless past,
found spotted all over with horrid fact
by the mere act
of questioning:
or found helplessly handling
my thing
at seventy
on a doorstep
wiping out a whole difficult lifetime
of dignity
and earning only the fascination
of passing
old women.

7

Not ceasing upon the midnight,
wakened by the heat
of abandoned crematory fires
or by vultures;

not being dead
as a tree under wood-
peckers plucking
out worms like nerves; with just enough
left to know

about vultures
and their unerring arts
of picking
on soft parts
like testicles and coconut brains.

8

I'll love my children
without end,
and do them infinite harm
staying on the roof,
a peeping-tom ghost
looking for all sorts of proof
for the presence of the past:

they'll serve a sentence
without any term
and know it only dimly
long afterwards
through borrowed words
and wrong analyses.

THE HINDOO: the Only Risk

Just to keep the heart's simple given beat
through a neighbour's striptease or a friend's suicide.
To keep one's hand away from the kitchen knife

through that returning weekly need
to maim oneself or carve up wife
and child. Always and everywhere, to eat

three square meals at regular hours; suppress
that itch to take a peek at the dead street-
dog before the scavengers come. Not to be caught

dead at sea, battle, riot, adultery or hate
nor between the rollers of a giant lathe. Yes,
to keep it cool when strangers' children hiss

as if they knew what none could know nor guess.
At the bottom of all this bottomless
enterprise to keep simple the heart's given beat,

the only risk is heartlessness.

REAL ESTATE

My cousin knows buildings;
he knows them well.
He can even tell
their gender by one look
at the basement.
Architect of our vertical
future, man of vision with a perfect
eye for parallax, he has compasses
in his rods and cones.
                      Where he is
there are cranes in the sky, pigeons
in the not-yet plaza.
                      He always knew
glass was good. 'It's rational,
it reflects',
enlisting attitudes of sky,
cloud, dazzle, aeroplanes,
for the man in the street;
filters images of the sun's
eclipse for the passerby;
                      yet refracts
all things for the man within,
defining some men in, others out,
with apparent transparency.

Humanist, he calculates
stress and strain on wood
and steel, on liver and lower brain.
When the lift gets stuck
in the marble quarry
or workmen go berserk
on the thirtieth floor,
his men collect within the hour

for the widows and the clerk
who lost his head in that altitude.

Yet he cannot exclude
the indiscipline of the second look
at mushrooms after rain
in the children's rooms, those
yellow thumbs in the reeking
crotches of rotting timber
bought years ago
for my uncle's
very carefully imagined
houses.
   Only we, our uncle's nephews, know
windows without walls
or the kinds of grass that grow
in the twinkle of an uncle's eye.

ANY COW'S HORN CAN DO IT

    Mention any cousin's death
in the walled red-fort city:
she'll weep aloud with no thought
of neighbours.
                Any reminder
of her youth's market places
crawling with feeling hands, eyes
groping for the hidden hooks
that hold together little girls
and she will glow green fire
from all nine wells of a woman's
shame.
           She'll grow cold remembering
what is not forgotten:
getting belted by father
standing on a doorstep
with a long strip of cowhide
and the family idiom
the day he caught her
in the hotel lobby,
                    mother's mouth
working red over betel leaf
and betelnut, the clove ground
into the nutmegs of satisfaction
seeing a disobedient daughter
brought to her senses.

    Any old quarrel over novel,
movie, or a suspicion
of pregnancy is enough
to make wife, sister, or girl friend
walk silent from room to room
smouldering with no care for burned
rice or the black nails of children

before visitors; a soreness
on two granules of her throat
will do it.
 Any number of things
can make a woman lie awake
and watch window-squares crawl out,
grow oblong and vanish
all night long with every car
in the street till morning's small
shadowless hour.

Any cow's horn tilted at
a child in the street will do it,
but nothing you say with words
in a poem will make her scream,
get sick, or go grey in the face.
You'll never do it, for poems
cannot flay like eyes or hurt
like a fall on a sidewalk,
cannot replace the panic
runs for imaginary
children in the middle room
of a house with the porch
on fire. Poems aren't even words
enough to rankle, infect
or make the smallest incisions
unless wife, girl friend or sister—

and I'm not talking of strangers
or the unborn—
 somehow are
made to think it's all about
their shame in the market, or
an elegy on the death
of a far-off cousin.

WHEN IT HAPPENS,

there will be surprises: mothers mean harm,
throw stepmother shadows on the woodwork.
Neither analysis, nor astrology

will help, but a virgin widow may bring
ripe papayas, a glass of pigeon's blood still warm,
a backdoor address in whorehouse alley.

Brothers practise circus knives, stand you between
identical alternative nightmares:
    wrench it out from its root in the belly,

    hook it out with a coat-hanger,
    flush it in the bathroom with *draino*
    like a careless pregnancy

    after a picnic with loafers. Yet you know
it has to be endured, be born head first,
licked into a likeness and a face,

every bit of the afterbirth eaten
before the strangers come with their compliments.
Or else a bulbous foetal eye

in formalin pickle will outstare
you from a schoolroom jar,
the twin vein on its sallow lid indigo

with age, when you Mother Superior go there
to give away prizes
to girlscouts and campfire girls.

SMALL-SCALE REFLECTIONS ON A GREAT HOUSE

Sometimes I think that nothing
that ever comes into this house
goes out. Things come in every day

to lose themselves among other things
lost long ago among
other things lost long ago;

lame wandering cows from nowhere
have been known to be tethered,
given a name, encouraged

to get pregnant in the broad daylight
of the street under the elders'
supervision, the girls hiding

behind windows with holes in them.

Unread library books
usually mature in two weeks
and begin to lay a row

of little eggs in the ledgers
for fines, as silverfish
in the old man's office room

breed dynasties among long legal words
in the succulence
of Victorian parchment.

Neighbours' dishes brought up
with the greasy sweets they made
all night the day before yesterday

for the wedding anniversary of a god,

never leave the house they enter,
like the servants, the phonographs,
the epilepsies in the blood,

sons-in-law who quite forget
their mothers, but stay to check
accounts or teach arithmetic to nieces,

or the women who come as wives
from houses open on one side
to rising suns, on another

to the setting, accustomed
to wait and to yield to monsoons
in the mountains' calendar

beating through the hanging banana leaves.

And also, anything that goes out
will come back, processed and often
with long bills attached,

like the hooped bales of cotton
shipped off to invisible Manchesters
and brought back milled and folded

for a price, cloth for our days'
middle-class loins, and muslin
for our richer nights. Letters mailed

have a way of finding their way back
with many re-directions to wrong
addresses and red ink marks

earned in Tiruvella and Sialkot.

And ideas behave like rumours,
once casually mentioned somewhere
they come back to the door as prodigies

born to prodigal fathers, with eyes
that vaguely look like our own,
like what Uncle said the other day:

that every Plotinus we read
is what some Alexander looted
between the malarial rivers.

A beggar once came with a violin
to croak out a prostitute song
that our voiceless cook sang

all the time in our backyard.

Nothing stays out: daughters
get married to short-lived idiots;
sons who run away come back

in grandchildren who recite Sanskrit
to approving old men, or bring
betelnuts for visiting uncles

who keep them gaping with
anecdotes of unseen fathers,
or to bring Ganges water

in a copper pot
for the last of the dying
ancestors' rattle in the throat.

And though many times from everywhere,

recently only twice:
once in nineteen-forty-three
from as far away as the Sahara,

half-gnawed by desert foxes,
and lately from somewhere
in the north, a nephew with stripes

on his shoulder was called
an incident on the border
and was brought back in plane

and train and military truck
even before the telegrams reached,
on a perfectly good

chatty afternoon.

SMALLTOWN, SOUTH INDIA

I return from the wide open spaces.
Temple employees have whiskered nipples.
The streetcows have trapezium faces.
Buffaloes shake off flies with a twitch of ripples.

I sink to the seabed in a barrel.
Water-layers salt and pickle the sun.
Toes mildew green, trees are porous coral:
ambush of city shark and wifely dolphin.

I bed down with long finless slipper fish.
The ceiling has weeds, the sleep is brackish.

SOME RELATIONS

1 *nursery turtles*

grounded here, carrying a daily cross
of window bars, an ordinary square
of sun, glowing and dimming with each cloud
up there:

      my daughter's turtles try
to hibernate in the jar, very far
from the ocean, beginning to be confused
by the heat of this Chicago winter

2 *kitten on tigerskin*

not yet fully recovered
from birth,
         blinking
blackwhite kitten yawn,
mew, make water
on a livingroom tigerskin
with green glass eyes
and shellac tongue

3 *a praying mantis*

a praying mantis, deathly still
on a yellow can of DDT
in the Madurai temple—

someone's cleaning out scorpions
from the many armpits of Shiva
one leg in the air

      broken by time
      or a passing Muslim
      from Ghazni

4 *in rem time*

my finger grows a lizard face
your pubic hair is tornado grass

my daughter's daughter's unborn face
floats to the surface: it has the natural

piety of the praying mantis
after a kill, its own or a butterfly's—

all over me are greenish
soft underbellies of ancestral

crocodiles and tortoises
the silent thud of their bloodbeat

—yet I do not shudder
at the coldness of their blood

TAKE CARE

In Chicago it blows
hot and cold. Trees
play fast and loose.
     Kittens and children
     have tics: the old
     have things in their
     eyes. So, do not breathe
deeply. Practise
analysis.
Invisible crabs
     scuttle the air.
     Small flies sit
     on aspirin and booze.
     Enemies have guns.
Friends have doubts.
Wives have lawyers.

Smudge your windows.
Draw the blinds.
All tall buildings
     use telescopes.
     Give daughters pills,
     learn karate.
     Prepare to get raped
bending for a book.
Go to the opera
in brown overalls,
     wear pure plastic
     on the daily bus.
     Think of the stink-
     bomb in the barber's
chair. Expect the knife
on the museum stair.

When you are there
take special care
not to stare
    at peppergrinders,
    salt shakers, or the box
    of matches on the black
    and white squares
of your kitchen cloth.
They take on the look
of meat grinders,
    cement shakers,
    boxes against boxes
    in the grilled
    city: intersections
of wet black splinter,
of houses burned

in the white oblongs
of winter, three T-
squares standing
    for the backstairs,
    the blacks black
    as the blacks
    in the Christmas snow
or the statistics
of City Hall
and Skid Row.
    In Chicago,
    do not walk slow.
    Find no time
    to stand and stare.
Down there, blacks look black.
And whites, they look blacker.

THE LAST OF THE PRINCES

They took their time to die, this dynasty
falling in slow motion from Aurangzeb's time:
some of bone TB,
others of a London fog that went to their heads,

some of current trends, imported wine and women,
one or two heroic in war or poverty,
with ballads
to their name. Father, uncles, seven

folklore brothers, sister so young so lovely
that snakes loved her and hung dead,
ancestral
lovers, from her ceiling; brother's many

wives, their unborn stillborn babies, numberless
cousins, royal mynahs and parrots
in the harem:
everyone died, to pass into his slow

conversation. He lives on, heir to long
fingers, faces in paintings, and a belief
in auspicious
snakes in the skylight: he lives on, to cough,

remember and sneeze, a balance of phlegm
and bile, alternating loose bowels and hard
sheep's pellets.
Two girls, Honey and Bunny, go to school

on half fees. Wife, heirloom pearl in her nose-ring,
pregnant again. His first son, trainee
in telegraphy,
has telegraphed thrice already for money.

OLD INDIAN BELIEF

        You need some

million ants with brief
methodical lives and calcium
limbs to build one ant-hill

and leave it in time
for the great recurring pattern
of the sudden snake.

No ant, red, white, or black,
can stand the smell
of a live cobra.

But they'll pick
the flesh off dead ones
to the last ivory rib:

with a little help
from rain, sun, and the natural
chemistry of recent flesh, they'll

leave snake skeletons
complete with fang and grin
for a schoolgirl's picnic

horror, and the local museum
collection of local celebrities.

HISTORY,

               which usually
changes slowly,
changes sometimes
during a single conversation:

the petite little aunt
in her garden of sweet limes
now carries a different
face, not merely older or colder
or made holy
by deaths and children's failures.

                             For instance
the day my great-aunt died
I was there by one of those
chances children never miss,
looking for a green ball
I never lost. I saw her
laid out, face incurious
eyes yet unshut,
between glass curio bureaus
under a naked cobweb bulb
next to a yellow dim window.

And my little dark aunt was there
—nose eyes and knee-bend cut
fresh from stone for a Parvati statue—
looking for something, half
her body under the cot,
maybe a rolling pin
her little son had brought for play
from under the kitchen mob
of cooking and washing relatives.

                                        But yesterday
my mother said, I've never told
anyone what happened
that day your great-aunt died:
with all those children in and out
of the death-room, all the kith and kin
milling in the kitchen, wet faggot smoke,
and rumours about the will,
                              her two
daughters, one dark one fair,
unknown each to the other
alternately picked their mother's body clean
before it was cold
or the eyes were shut,
     of diamond ear-rings,
     bangles, anklets, the pin
     in her hair,
     the toe-rings from her wedding
     the previous century,
     all except the gold
     in her teeth and the silver g-string
     they didn't know she wore
     her napkins on
     to the great disgust
     of the orthodox widows
     who washed her body
     at the end,

and the dark
stone face of my little aunt
acquired some expression
at last.

COMPENSATIONS

I've even heard of surviving
World War men with wooden legs
doing cha cha cha's and jitterbugs
at Army Hospitals, near debris
and craters, especially
outside the amputation theatres;

the dumb and the colourblind rise
rapidly in politics; the born deaf
practise psychiatry as if
to the practice born; fingerless
men become tailors for royalty,
painters, filigree workers in

silver, or excel at the javelin
throw; with a hook for a hand
men hold and pull black strings
in a puppetshow or a boxing
syndicate; stutterers become salesmen
for things like machine guns

or pet woodpeckers; good
upstanding men deformed
by literacy abroad
return middle-aged to farming
and the innocence of knowing
a spade for a spade and a bird

for a bird, learning without
the benefit of names and forms
the works and the days, the signs
of fevers, madness and the rains:
miracles of vengeful reversal
like some spinsters' need to succeed

only as hydraulic engineers
in swarming barren lands, or the great
familiar men falling apart in state,
holding together, entire,
the ancient chaos of a country
by barely living on in a high chair

that ought to have wheels, renewing
honesty by their cunning, reviving
failing youth by just dying
at the wrong time, at the aimless
hand of an assassin, at the mercy
of a watch that ran too fast—

surpassed only by the last
miracle of grace, the three-eyed
whirlwind of arms, dancing on
a single leg though he can dance
on many, kind returning god
of Indian deluges,

dying from time to time
of sheer fatigue, leaving
the technicalities of war,
famine, riot and the rest
to us, two-handed two-legged normal us,
in a periodic transfer of powers.

OBITUARY

Father, when he passed on,
left dust
on a table full of papers,
left debts and daughters,
a bedwetting grandson
named by the toss
of a coin after him,

a house that leaned
slowly through our growing
years on a bent coconut
tree in the yard.
Being the burning type,
he burned properly
at the cremation

as before, easily
and at both ends,
left his eye coins
in the ashes that didn't
look one bit different,
several spinal discs, rough,
some burned to coal, for sons

to pick gingerly
and throw as the priest
said, facing east
where three rivers met
near the railway station;
no longstanding headstone
with his full name and two dates

to hold in their parentheses
everything he didn't quite

manage to do himself,
like his caesarian birth
in a brahmin ghetto
and his death by heart-
failure in the fruit market.

But someone told me
he got two lines
in an inside column
of a Madras newspaper
sold by the kilo
exactly four weeks later
to streethawkers

who sell it in turn
to the small groceries
where I buy salt,
coriander,
and jaggery
in newspaper cones
that I usually read

for fun, and lately
in the hope of finding
these obituary lines.
And he left us
a changed mother
and more than
one annual ritual.

PRAYERS TO LORD MURUGAN*

1

Lord of new arrivals
lovers and rivals:
arrive
at once with cockfight and banner-
dance till on this and the next three
hills

women's hands and the garlands
on the chests of men will turn like
chariotwheels

O where are the cockscombs and where
the beaks glinting with new knives
at crossroads

when will orange banners burn
among blue trumpet flowers and the shade
of trees

waiting for lightnings?

2

Twelve etched arrowheads
for eyes and six unforeseen
faces, and you were not
embarrassed.

Unlike other gods
you found work
for every face,
and made

---

* Ancient Dravidian god of fertility, joy, youth, beauty, war, and love. He is represented as a six-faced god with twelve hands.

eyes at only one
woman. And your arms
are like faces with proper
names.

3

Lord of green
growing things, give us
a hand

in our fight
with the fruit fly.
Tell us,

will the red flower ever
come to the branches
of the blueprint

city?

4

Lord of great changes and small
cells: exchange our painted grey
pottery

for iron copper the leap of stone horses
our yellow grass and lily seed
for rams'

flesh and scarlet rice for the carnivals
on rivers O dawn of nightmare virgins
bring us

your white-haired witches who wear
three colours even in sleep.

5

Lord of the spoor of the tigress,
outside our town hyenas
and civet cats live
on the kills of leopards
and tigers

too weak to finish what's begun.
Rajahs stand in photographs
over ninefoot silken tigresses
that sycophants have shot.
Sleeping under country fans

hearts are worm cans
turning over continually
for the great shadows
of fish in the open
waters.

We eat legends and leavings,
remember the ivory, the apes,
the peacocks we sent in the Bible
to Solomon, the medicines for smallpox,
the similes

for muslin: wavering snakeskins,
a cloud of steam.
Ever-rehearsing astronauts,
we purify and return
our urine

to the circling body
and burn our faeces
for fuel to reach the moon
through the sky behind
the navel.

6

Master of red bloodstains,
our blood is brown;
our collars white.

Other lives and sixty-
four rumoured arts
tingle,

pins and needles
at amputees' fingertips
in phantom muscle.

7

Lord of the twelve right hands
why are we your mirror men
with the two left hands

capable only of casting
reflections? Lord
of faces,

find us the face
we lost early
this morning.